The Library of American Choreographers™

JOSÉ LIMÓN

Jennifer Cady

rosen central™

The Rosen Publishing Group, Inc., New York

Published in 2006 by The Rosen Publishing Group, Inc.
29 East 21st Street, New York, NY 10010

First Edition

Library of Congress Cataloging-in-Publication Data

Cady, Jennifer.
José Limón / Jennifer Cady.
p. cm. — (The library of American choreographers)
Includes bibliographical references.
ISBN 1-4042-0449-0 (lib. bdg.)
ISBN 1-4042-0643-4 (pbk. bdg.)
1. Limón, José—Juvenile literature. 2. Dancers—United States—Biography—Juvenile literature. 3. Choreographers—United States—Biography—Juvenile literature.
I. Title. II. Series.
GV1785.L515C33 2006
792.8'092—dc22

2005000922

Manufactured in the United States of America

Cover: Inset: José Limón, circa 1960. Background: Four male dancers in Limón's company perform "A Time to Plant," from *There is a Time*, circa 1956.

Contents

Introduction

José Limón was born and raised in Mexico. When he moved to the United States as a child, he had dreams inside of him that he was not even aware of just yet. Not until he saw a dance performance did he know what his American dream was going to be. He would become one of America's most respected and well-known dancers and choreographers.

Not only is he remembered as a great dancer and choreographer, he is also known as a creator of a new dance technique. During his more than forty years of life as a dancer, José Limón developed his own way of moving and dancing called the Limón Technique. Many dancers throughout the world study his technique now.

Limón performed and choreographed all over the world. He created many dances, including *The Moor's Pavane* (1949). This piece is considered by many dance histo-

Lucas Hoving, José Limón, and Betty Jones in *The Moor's Pavane* (1949). Not pictured is Pauline Koner. On the tenth anniversary of its premiere, Limón wrote a letter to these original cast members in which he described how *The Moor's Pavane* remains fresh, challenging, and exciting to perform.

rians and critics to be a near-perfect work of art. Many ballet and modern dance companies have performed it ever since. Even today it continues to move audiences through its exquisite harmony of form and content.

Carrying his childhood experiences with him from Mexico, José Limón would move to the United States and make his American dream come true. He would break new ground in the world of modern dance.

1 The Early Years

José Arcadia Limón was born on January 12, 1908, in Culiacán, the capital of the state of Sinaloa in Mexico. Culiacán is one of Mexico's largest cities, and when José was a very young boy, the city thrived. Yet within a short time of young José's life, the city would fall to economic struggles. This would have a major impact on the social status of middle-class families such as José's.

Florencio Limón, José's father, was a musician and conductor. He played the clarinet and cello, and taught young José how to play the organ. José loved to play the music of Johann Sebastian Bach on the organ. Later in his life, he would often choreograph to Bach's music.

Limón's mother was Francisca Traslavina. Her family had roots of Yaqui Indian blood. José Limón was the oldest of eleven brothers and sisters. Four of his brothers and sisters died during birth or at a very young age. The

José (standing) is pictured here with his mother Francisca, and his younger siblings. By sixth grade, José was considered the artist of the family. He often drew for his younger brothers and sisters.

many difficult pregnancies caused his mother to die at the early age of thirty-four. José was only eighteen years old when his mother died.

By nature, José was a shy, quiet child growing up. He had dark, deep eyes, a strong muscular face, and a mane of thick dark hair.

Education and the family's social status were very important in the Limón household. José and his siblings had a rather formal upbringing, even speaking a very proper version of Spanish at home. José began school in Mexico, where he learned the alphabet, numbers, and some basic arithmetic. In his autobiography, *An Unfinished Memoir* (1999), he recalls his few childhood memories of school. His favorite teachers were those who used games that made learning interesting and fun. Later in his life, when he taught dance, he used a style of discipline similar to what he first learned in elementary school.

The Mexican Revolution

In 1915, when José was seven years old, his father decided the family had to leave Mexico. Many reasons forced this decision, all resulting from the Mexican Revolution of 1910. It became very difficult and dangerous to live in Mexico. One morning while eating breakfast, the family heard what they first thought were firecrackers. When José's uncle looked out the window to view what was happening, he was shot and killed. José and his family witnessed this horrific event.

Many schools in Mexico began to close. Soon, this included the Academia de Musica where José's father worked. The family decided to immigrate to the United States.

Moving to the United States was not an easy task. Later in his adult life, Limón would recall vivid memories of the terror and anguish his family endured on the long train ride from Mexico. His younger brother Gilberto became very ill on the journey, and Limón witnessed soldiers executing a man at one of the train stops. These memories would stay with José. After briefly settling in

Mexican rebels enter the captured city of Sinalra in 1913, the same year they would capture José's hometown of Cananea. The revolution began in 1910, with an uprising against the dictatorship of Mexico's president, Porfirio Diaz. The peasants sought to end years of oppression.

Tucson, Arizona, the family moved to Los Angeles, California. José stayed in California until shortly after he started college.

Although José left Mexico at the early age of seven, the country would continue to have a profound effect on his life. Indeed, this was where he had witnessed the horrific murder of his uncle. It was where his father introduced him to the world of music. It was in Mexico he learned about his own peoples, both Spanish and Native American, whose cultures he would later celebrate in his choreography. The next time José would be in Mexico would be the year 1951, as an accomplished performer and choreographer.

Living in America

As a kid, José only spoke Spanish. The only English he had ever encountered before starting school in America was on signs in Mexico. Once he began speaking English, he helped his father learn the language. Not comfortable with feeling like an "outsider" in his new home country, José became determined to master the English language. Eventually José could speak and write English better than many Americans around him.

José was an excellent student in high school. He liked exploring and discovering new things, especially the arts. Art classes, music, and poetry were some of his favorite areas of study.

José had some teachers who were very important to him. They inspired him to learn and become an artist. Miss Myrta Herbert was José's art teacher in high school. She introduced him to painters such as Rembrandt, Manet, and Picasso. Miss Reta Mitchell, his choral singing teacher, helped him study the piano.

Both these teachers guided and helped shape the artist José became later in his life.

In 1926, José graduated from high school. He enrolled at the University of California, Los Angeles, to study painting. There, he met three friends who inspired him as an artist. Don Forbes, Fernando Felix, and Perkins Harnly introduced José to contemporary and avant-garde art. The friends would all hang out in their studios, listening to music, reading books, and discussing their dreams of becoming artists. In the early fall of 1928, José moved to New York City to follow his friends and his dream of becoming a painter.

Discovering Modern Dance

Once in New York City, Limón became artistically disillusioned. He wanted to paint with the best painters, but at that time, most of them were moving to France to paint. It also seemed that many aspiring painters around him were simply imitating the work of others. Although Limón himself was moved by El Greco, he felt that this innovative painter had already accomplished what Limón would have wanted to do. Soon, José was left in New York City without clear goals and working as an elevator operator and a janitor in order to make a living. However, an event was about to unfold that would change his life and the modern dance world forever.

One evening in 1929, Limón and his friends went to see a performance of a German dancer named Harald Kreutzberg. Limón had never seen a man move the way Kreutzberg did on stage. Kreutzberg performed strong movements that expressed an emotional story. Limón was so impressed that he decided to stop

The New Life in Dance Class

In his book, , *An Unfinished Memoir* Limón recalls his dance classes at the Humphrey-Weidman Studio. He says, "Doris Humphrey makes you do things you have never done before. You stretch; you bend and flex your legs, your arches and torso, every muscle, tendon, nerve, vein, and artery—all of you, your whole entire you. You run, jump, and turn; you fall to the floor and rise again. From the piano where sits Pauline comes Bach and Chopin, Brahms and Henry Cowell. You pant, sweat and hurt. You learn that you are. You learn that the past—the jarabes, the bullfights, the painting, the Mexican in you, the fearful passage to the land of the gringos, the wounds, the deaths—have been only a preparation for this new life."

painting and start dancing.

The type of dance that José saw that evening is called modern dance. There are many styles of modern dance. The style danced by Harald Kreutzberg is called German expressionism. It is related to ballet technique but uses movement to express emotions and tell stories in abstract and unique ways.

At that time, modern dance was just beginning to develop in America. Just by chance, Limón's friends Don Forbes and Perkins Harnly were good friends of Charles Weidman, one of the pioneers of American modern dance. They introduced Limón to him. Soon after, Limón began taking dance classes with Charles Weidman and his dancing partner, Doris Humph- rey, at the Humphrey-Weidman Studio.

2 Finding His Place in Dance

Doris Humphrey and Charles Weidman were two of the best teachers in all of America at that time. These two dancers had just recently left the Denishawn Company. Before that, they had trained at the Denishawn School, considered by most dance historians to be the first modern dance school in America.

Ruth St. Denis and her husband, Ted Shawn, founded the Denishawn Company and the Denishawn School. Together with Isadora Duncan, these three important artists are considered the first generation of modern dancers in America. At Denishawn, the students were trained in various forms of dance such as ballet, ballroom, lyrical, and the native and classical dances of many different countries. Yet some Denishawn students, including Humphrey, Weidman, and Martha Graham, felt that these dances did not let them dance as themselves as

Martha Graham and Charles Weidman perform a piece choreographed by Graham, circa 1930. The stark geometric shape of this pose was typical of Graham's style at this time.

Americans. They wanted more from dance. They wanted to express themes more directly connected to their lives. They wanted to find a form of dance that would reflect their heritage as Americans.

Humphrey and Weidman left Denishawn to start their own school and company in New York City. At that time, Martha Graham was also starting her company. In 1928 the Humphrey-Weidman Company was the only modern dance company with an ensemble of both men and women dancers.

Taking Class

Classes with Doris Humphrey and Charles Weidman were quite an adventure! During the classes they were each exploring different ways to move. Doris Humphrey was exploring principles of breathing and relating to gravity. She taught exercises based on gravity and how to fall onto and then recover from the floor. She taught how to use breath to suspend a movement or shape a movement phrase. Charles Weidman was exploring how gestures and pantomime could be used in new, abstract ways to create character and comedy in dance.

Limón liked exploring movement as well as the emotional and storytelling sides of modern dance. Dance classes not only taught him technique, they began to teach him who he was and what he was capable of doing. The shy, quiet José became the "mad stallion in human form," as his codancer, Nona Schurman, put it. Indeed, Limón tapped into the pain, anger, and oppression that he experienced in his life, and everyone around him saw that he could powerfully convey these emotions through movement.

Limón found Weidman's teaching to be a great deal of fun even though it was sometimes difficult for him. Because Limón was more of a private, quiet man, he felt silly doing Weidman's pantomimes and games. Later in his career, he realized it was good that he learned how to express humor through his dancing. Charles Weidman helped Limón see when his first works were too serious. Although José wanted his dances to be about meaningful topics such as war, betrayal, and pain, he did not want his dances to be pretentious. By exploring both comedic and dramatic extremes, he was able to figure out the balance needed to effectively tell his stories.

Limón did not start dancing until the age of twenty. Most dancers usually have years of technique behind them by that age. Because of Limón's late start, Doris Humphrey did not at first think he would make a good dancer. But Limón worked very hard at improving his strength and flexibility. By 1931, after only three years with the company, Doris began letting him perform solos—the best compliment a choreographer can give a dancer. She saw that he had the will and passion for dance and trusted him with the entire stage.

Limón Performs

After working many long hours in and out of the studio, José Limón made his debut with the Humphrey-Weidman Company in its performance at the Guild Theatre in New York City in 1928. The program consisted of small ensemble works including *Concert in A Minor*, choreographed by Humphrey. Limón had a very simple part in a dance by Charles Weidman called *Javanese Impressions*. Still, he was nervous and kept checking his costume. In his memoir, he mentions his debut experience as a taste of "true terror and

Charles Weidman, Doris Humphrey, and José Limón dance *Exhibition in Piece,* 1939. Limón was ecstatic when he was approached by his mentors to be the third dancer in this comedic piece. Much to Limón's amazement, he found his talent for comedy in it.

undreamed exaltation, humility and triumph."

Once José Limón began dancing, he never stopped. From 1928 to 1940, he danced with the Humphrey-Weidman Company and performed in some of its most well-known dances. These include *Water Study* (1928), *The Shakers* (1931), *New Dance: Variations and Conclusion* (1935), and *Passacaglia and Fugue in C Minor* (1938), all choreographed by Humphrey.

Water Study, set in silence, conjures up a variety of sea moods ranging from calm to tidal and wind-driven turbulence. Unlike most dances of that time, this dance does not rely on numerical counting to create or maintain its structure. Instead, the dancers synchronized all their movements by learning to breathe together as an ensemble. *The Shakers* is about how religious purification is achieved through delight in the American religious community of Shakers. Here, the dancers begin with small trembling gestures that become larger shaking movements, conjuring the emotion of extreme bliss.

New Dance: Variations and Conclusion represents a democratic world where each person has a clear and harmonious relationship with his or her fellow beings. When Charles Weidman began to retire from performing, Humphrey chose Limón to replace him in *Passacaglia and Fugue in C Minor*, which was a huge honor. This dance is a vision of an ideal world where people live in peaceful harmony with one another. Both of these dances are considered masterpieces of American modern dance. They are also examples of Humphrey's interest in using pure form and mass dynamics to express content.

Other prominent works by Humphrey following this period of great success included *Day on Earth*, *Night Spell*, and *Ritmo Jondo*. In 1947, José Limón starred in *Day on Earth* as the everyman experiencing the age-old cycle of work, love, birth, loss, companionship, death, and continuation. *Night Spell*, choreographed in 1951, is inspired by the poems "I Hear an Army" by D. H. Lawrence and "Dover Beach" by Matthew Arnold. In this dance, a sleeper is tormented by dreams and dream figures that emerge from his sub-conscious. Through all the terror, the sleeper prevails because of his embrace of a single image of love that appears to him. The third well-known piece, *Ritmo Jondo*, was choreographed in 1953. It paints a portrait of men and women as they meet and part. To alluring Spanish rhythms, a band of assertive males presents themselves to a group of female admirers. They court them with sweeping gestures and then they leave them to attend to matters that are more urgent. The women keep to swirling and loose gestures while the men use more direct, thrusting steps.

Dance and Universities

One major accomplishment of Doris Humphrey that would become just as important to Limón was gaining recognition for modern dance in colleges and universities. She and Charles Weidman believed that dance was an art form equal to music and belonged in the schools. This was not easy: at the time, many educators believed dance did not belong in colleges and universities. They did not understand the value of the craft and techniques of modern dance and thought all dance should stay in the studios and conservatories. Humphrey also contributed to dance education with *The Art of Making Dances*, published in 1959. The first book in English on the technique of choreography, it remains an essential book on choreographic principles.

When colleges became familiar with Humphrey's teaching and choreography, they began hiring Limón as well. Bennington College, Temple University, the University of Pittsburgh, Colorado State College of Education, and the University of California at Berkley were just a few of the many colleges at which Limón taught and made dances in the 1930s. The students benefited from the experience of working with a disciplined and talented artist, and Limón in turn benefited from a steady paycheck and the opportunity to develop his art when teaching.

Pauline Lawrence

In 1927, Pauline Lawrence became the pianist for the Humphrey-Weidman Company, playing for classes and rehearsals. She was also a costume designer, a lighting expert, and a publicity agent for the company. Lawrence added another important role later in her life. On October 3, 1941, José Limón and Pauline Lawrence were married in San Francisco. She would also become manager for José Limón's dance company.

Becoming a Choreographer

In addition to his dance technique classes, Limón studied dance composition with Doris Humphrey and Charles Weidman. Limón had many chances to choreograph and show his dances while he was studying and performing with them at their Studio Theater in New York City, and during their many residences at colleges across America. Limón took every chance he got to choreograph and work on new pieces.

Danzas Mexicanas, his first major choreographic work, was created in 1939 during a residency at Mills College in Oakland, California. This suite of five short dances presented the many layers of Mexican history through the dance of a solo male figure. Each of the dances had a Spanish title and elements of Spanish or Native American dress in the costume. In the first dance, entitled "Indio" in Spanish or "Indian" in English, Limón was an indigenous person, warm and connected to the earth. In "Conquistador," the second dance, he became a proud but brutal Spanish conqueror. In the third dance, "Peon," José was a sad, enslaved native person. In "Caballero," his romantic, elegant attitude mixed with an undertone of cruelty returned as José became a gentleman landowner or land-grabber. And finally in "Revolutionario," José became a revolutionary similar to the type who took part in the Mexican Revolution that he had witnessed in his youth.

In 1942, he created another one of his best-known and most important dances, *Chaconne*. It is also a solo, composed to the *Chaconne* in D Minor by J. S. Bach. The chaconne is an ancient dance form thought to have originated in Mexico. It eventually became a social dance in the aristocratic courts of Europe during the sixteenth and seventeenth centuries. Limón's pure dance version beautifully captured the essence of his native land and the form and spirit of the music by his favorite composer.

Limón is pictured here in *Chaconne*, 1942. When choreographing this piece for himself, Limón locked himself up in a room and let the music take command and dictate to him how to move. The resulting dance was majestic, formal, and elegant.

Limón's Army Years

In March 1943, America was fighting in World War II (1939–1945) and Limón was drafted into the army. He spent most of his thirty-two months of military service choreographing, directing, and performing for Special Services. Because the shows were primarily used to entertain the troops or raise money for the war effort, he had the opportunity to expand his stylistic range. The performances included everything from burlesque variety-type shows to nativity pageants. During his off-hours, he rehearsed for modern dance concerts that he performed in his time off from the army.

During these years in the army, Limón began to

worry that his career as a modern dancer and choreographer might end. However, when he returned to civilian life, he was more determined than ever to begin something new in the dance world. Limón later recalled in his September 1, 1959 "Letter to Pauline, Betty, and Lucas on the occasion of the 10th Anniversary of The Moor's Pavane:" "I was thirty-seven years old. The years in the Army had meant for me

José Limón dances in "We Speak for Ourselves" from *Fun for the Birds* _ (1943) at Camp Lee, Virginia, one of the pieces he choreographed for Special Services. Limón used soldiers with no dance training for the piece; the result confirmed his belief that all people have a natural dance instinct.

Limón on Broadway

José Limón performed and choreographed for many years, on many stages. He even had the chance to perform on Broadway. In 1930, Limón performed in Norman Bel Geddes' Broadway production of *Lysistrata,* choreographed by Doris Humphrey and Charles Weidman. Also that year, he was in the musical revue *Americana*, which featured dances by Humphrey and Weidman, and Irving Berlin's *As Thousands Cheer.* He also appeared on Broadway in the leading dance role of *Rosalinda.*

an inevitable retrogression as a dancer. I could accept this and turn to something else, or I could work harder than ever and get myself back. I chose the latter course." Limón was discharged in 1945, and he became a U.S. citizen in 1947.

3 Creating the José Limón Dance Company

In 1946, Limón formed his own dance company. Because he loved dancing as much as he loved choreographing, he asked his teacher Doris Humphrey to be the artistic director and co-choreographer of his company. This was an unusual choice. At that time, and even today, most modern dancers form a company just to present their own choreography. But Limón respected Humphrey's work. He wanted to continue to dance for her and to help bring her dances to life onstage.

One year later, on January 5, 1947, the José Limón Dance Company had its debut performance at New York City's Belasco Theatre. The program included two dances by Limón, *Chaconne* and *Concerto Grosso*, and two dances choreographed by Doris Humphrey specifically for Limón, *Lament for Ignacio Sanchez Mejias*, based on the poem by Federico García Lorca with original music

Limón as the Bullfighter in *Lament for Ignacio Sanchez Mejias*. In addition to the Bullfighter, the piece also included characters called Witness and Mourner and the Guardian of Destiny.

composed by Norman Lloyd, and *The Story of Mankind*. *Lament for Ignacio Sanchez Mejias* tells the tragic story of one of Spain's most famous bullfighters. Humphrey's notes for this piece state that Limón's character "is intended to signify the struggle of all men of courage who contend in the ring of life and who meet a tragic end." Limón recalls in his *An Unfinished Memoir*, "the show was a huge success. The audience gave us a reception I shall never forget." The *New York Times* reported that Limón was "the finest male dancer of his time." José Limón was on his way to becoming one of America's most accomplished male dancers and choreographers.

Sadly, even with this success, life as a dancer and choreographer was financially difficult for Limón in the 1940s. Teaching and performing at dance festivals became an important financial and creative opportunity for the José Limón Dance Company, just as they had been for the Humphrey-Weidman Company. In 1948, the company performed at the first American Dance Festival held at Connecticut College. From 1948 until 1973, José Limón and his company taught and danced every year at this festival.

The Moor's Pavane

Many choreographers have based dances on the plays of William Shakespeare. On August 17, 1949, Limón premiered his creation *The Moor's Pavane* at the second annual American Dance Festival at Connecticut College. This dance is based on Shakespeare's *Othello*.

The Theme

Also known as *The Moor of Venice*, *Othello* is a tragic story of love and honor, jealousy and deception, and pride and prejudice. "Moor" is a word that describes people of a particular mixed African and Arab heritage, much like the way "Native American" describes the indigenous people of America. In the story, the moor is Othello, a successful mercenary soldier in service to the Duke of Venice. Othello woos and weds Desdemona, the beautiful daughter of a wealthy Venetian merchant. Iago, an ensign in service to Othello, is envious and prejudiced against him. Iago devises a deceitful scheme that causes Othello to doubt Desdemona's true love for him. Eventually, Othello becomes so jealous that he kills Desdemona. In the end, Emilia, Iago's wife and Desdemona's servant, reveals the truth of Iago's evil plan. In grief and horror, Othello takes his own life as Iago is taken off to trial.

Style of the Dance

Although there are many characters in Shakespeare's play, Limón's dance has just four: the two couples of Othello and Desdemona, and Iago and Emilia. Limón used the pavane, a sixteenth-century European court dance performed by couples, as the basis for the structure of his dance. He found the formal design of the pavane rich with patterns and shapes that he could manipulate to show the secret relationships of the characters.

The costumes, created by Limón's wife Pauline Lawrence, were courtly dress attire. The women wore large layered dresses while the men wore jacket and pant sets. The music was titled *The Moor's Revenge*, by seventeenth-century English composer Henry Purcell, and arranged by Simon Sadoff.

Limón danced the role of the moor. Betty

Jones danced Desdemona; Lucas Hoving was Iago; and Pauline Koner played Emilia. Although the dance has a small cast, it has a large emotional impact on the audience. These great dancers helped make the dance so powerful. When dance critic Clive Barnes saw the original production, he stated in the *New York Times* that *The Moor's Pavane* was

The two couples of *The Moor's Pavane* are pictured here: Pauline Koner, Lucas Hoving, Limón, and Betty Jones. Each interaction between the four dancers, present on stage for the entire piece, brings about a dramatic change to the symmetry of this court-like dance.

a "dance of truly Shakespearean dimension."

The Moor's Pavane is a masterpiece that remains one of the most widely performed modern dances in the world. Not only has the José Limón Dance Company performed this piece many times in many places, other companies all over the world have bought the rights to perform this dance.

Other Well-Known Choreography

The Traitor, created in 1954, is set against a musical score of violence, passion, and tenderness written by Gunther Schuller. It portrays the tragedy of Judas as if it were taking place in modern times. José Limón's program note explains it best: "The arch-betrayer, Judas Iscariot, is used in this work to symbolize all those tormented men who, loving too much, must hate: these men who, to our own day, must turn against their loyalties, friends and fatherlands, and in some fearful cataclysm of the spirit, betray them to the enemy."

There Is a Time, created in 1956, is a work choreographed and composed with a theme and variation method using circular pathways. It is based on the well-known verses from chapter 3 of Ecclesiastes, a book of the Bible. It begins with, "to every thing there is a season, and a time to every purpose under heaven." Limón uses the circle as a recurring motif throughout the choreography. The continual use of circles represents the idea that time itself is never ending. Within a period of time, things change as seasons do, but time itself is eternal. The original working title, *Variations on a Theme,* reinforces the idea of time and change. The musical score by composer Norman Dello Joio, *Meditations on Ecclesiastes*, earned a Pulitzer Prize. *There Is a Time* clearly reflects the musicality that is characteristic of Limón's work.

While on a European tour during 1957, Limón spent a lot of time performing in Poland. He viewed firsthand the bravery of the Polish people as they rebuilt their country after the devastation of World War II. He was so moved by how strong they were and how passionate they were to express their own identity, he choreographed a piece based on this experience. The dance *Missa Brevis* was set to an existing score by Zoltán Kodály titled *Missa Brevis in Tempore Belli* meaning "mass in time of war." The music was originally composed in 1945. In the dance, Limón is a central figure, always watching the faithful people of Poland. Although Limón desired to join the people,

Shakespeare as Dance

The works of William Shakespeare have inspired many dances. By far, *Romeo and Juliet* is the play that has been used most often. The first version was choreographed by Evsebio Luzzi in Venice in 1785. Many twentieth-century choreographers have reinterpreted the play using the three-act score composed by Sergei Prokofiev (1891–1953) that premiered in 1938. These choreographers include Leonid Lavrovsky for the Kirov Ballet in 1940 and for the Bolshoi Ballet in 1946 (both located in Russia). John Cranko choreographed the ballet in 1958 for La Scala Ballet in Italy and later in 1962 for the Stuttgart Ballet in Germany. Kenneth MacMillan choreographed a version of the play in 1965 for the Royal Ballet in England. The very first of Shakespeare's plays to be adapted for dance was *Antony and Cleopatra,* choreographed by Jean-George Noverre in Stuttgart, Germany, in 1761. Salvatore Viganò's *Othello* made its debut in Milan, Italy, in 1818. Yet perhaps the most famous are George Balanchine's full-length *A Midsummer Night's Dream* for the New York City Ballet, which debuted in 1964, followed by Sir Frederick Ashton's *The Dream,* a one-act ballet based on a scene from the same play, made for the Royal Ballet, also in 1964. The most recent version of *Othello* was choreographed by Lar Lubovitch for American Ballet Theatre and the San Francisco Ballet in 1997.

he did not feel right joining. He was in a constant struggle as to what he should do. In his *New York Times* review, John Martin writes, "His use of the group as a group is a natural outgrowth of the subject and the material; when the individual emerges he is nonetheless an individual, and when he takes his personal flashes of emotional realization back into the group he is no less a part of the group. There is a remarkable awareness of the solitude of the individual, and yet also of the group as something more than a mere aggregation of solitudes."

Limón's *The Winged*, choreographed in 1966, was originally set for twenty-eight dancers and, like Humphrey's *Water Story* that Limón had danced many years before, performed in complete silence. The choreographic gestures and movements were inspired by the flight and behavior of birds. This piece imitates various rituals of birds as they soar in the air, flurry on the ground, mate, and even combat each other.

Psalm, choreographed in 1967, is a piece inspired by a Jewish legend. In this piece, one man unknowingly carries the sorrows of the world upon his shoulders. The choreography captures the isolation, anguish, and ultimate redemption of the "just man" as he moves through a symbolic landscape of ritual, history, and belief.

The Unsung, choreographed in 1970, is one of Limón's last pieces. It is a tribute to the spirit and nobility of Native Americans. It assembles many great Native American chiefs, including Sitting Bull, Tecumseh, and Osceola. This piece builds as the chiefs gather from various places and share through movement stories of where they have been and their trials. Performed by the men of the company to no accompaniment other than the sounds of stamping, running, leaping, and breathing, the choreography is stunning in its invention and gripping in its impact.

4 Recognition at Home and Abroad

With the great success of *The Moor's Pavane* and his other choreography, opportunities began to arise quickly for José Limón and his company. In 1954, the José Limón Dance Company inaugurated the U.S. State Department's International Exchange Program with a tour to South America. It was the first dance company to be sent abroad on a cultural mission by the United States State Department. Soon it toured other international destinations. It went to Europe in 1957, South and Central America in 1960, and the Far East and Australia in 1963. In 1973, just after Limón's death, the company went to Russia.

In 1963, the José Limón Dance Company was the first dance company to perform at Philharmonic Hall (now Avery Fisher Hall) in the brand-new arts complex called Lincoln Center in New York. In 1964, Limón was appointed the director of Lincoln

Limón and company member Ruth Currier perform *Day on Earth*, choreographed by Doris Humphrey in 1947.

Center's American Dance Theatre, the first publicly supported modern dance repertory company. In 1965, the original cast of *The Moor's Pavane* was invited to perform at the White House for the Lyndon B. Johnson administration.

In 1969, other major dance companies began presenting Limón's dances. Limón was invited to set *The Moor's Pavane* and *The Traitor* on American Ballet Theatre. In that same year, the Royal Swedish Ballet presented an entire program of Limón's work. Other famous ballet companies that have performed his works include the Joffrey Ballet, the Pennsylvania Ballet, and Les Grands Ballets Canadiens.

The Limón Technique and Repertory

José Limón was not only a great dancer and choreographer. Like his mentors Doris Humphrey and Charles Weidman, he was also a great teacher. He taught in the dance division at The Julliard School of Music in New York City for more than twenty years, in addition to guest teaching at festivals throughout the world. Just like his own teachers, Limón did not settle for simply teaching what he had previously learned. He explored the basic principles of movement to develop his technique and style of dancing. Much of the Limón Technique builds on the work of Doris Humphrey in its use of breath and gravity to create a fluid, dynamic movement style. By using the weight of the body as an expressive element, Limón was able to communicate a range of emotions in his dances. He created dozens of athletic, physically demanding works that built on Humphrey's principle of fall and recovery, and referred to literature, history, and current events.

Through exploration of the body and its ability to tell a story, José Limón often told stories of his past in his choreography. He recalled people such as the bullfighters and Native Americans, or events he witnessed, such as his uncle being killed in Mexico. He discovered a way to communicate deep feelings through dance.

Awards and Honors

José Limón received two Dance Magazine Awards. His first was awarded to him in 1950, for choreographing *The Moor's Pavane*. His second Dance Magazine Award was presented to him in 1957. In 1964, he received a Capezio Dance Award. He also received honorary doctorates from Wesleyan University, Colby College, the University of North Carolina, and Oberlin College in acknowledgment of his achievements.

In the fall of 1996, the New York Public Library for the Performing Arts hosted an exhibition entitled, *The Dance Heroes of José Limón*. And in 1997 José Limón was inducted into the Hall of Fame at the National Museum of Dance in Saratoga Springs, New York.

A Full Life Comes to an End

José Limón was an important part of the dance world for more than forty years. He kept dancing until 1969 when he was sixty-one years old. In fact, after he stopped dancing, he still choreographed up until the year of his death. He premiered his final work, *Carlota*, before dying of cancer in 1972. From 1949 to 1972, he choreographed at least one new piece each year. In total, he choreographed seventy-four dances.

His Legacy Lives On

One of José Limón's greatest accomplishments is the endurance of his dance company. Limón was the

Limón is pictured here on January 27, 1958, with Lucia Chase, Alicia Markova, and Jerome Robbins, all Dance Magazine Award winners for 1957. This was Limón's second Dance Magazine Award. Dance Magazine recognizes and honors a wide range of dance professionals.

first modern dancer to form a dance company that remained as a performing entity after the death of its founder. In the past, when someone created a dance company, the company ended when the founder retired or passed away. The José Limón Dance Foundation, founded in 1968 by Limón's dancers and admirers, oversees two programs that preserve his technique and dances. There is the Limón Institute, serving as an educational and archival resource by safeguarding the words and pictures that document the dances. And there is the José Limón Dance Company, now simply called the Limón Dance Company.

Today, audiences can still observe Limón's masterful work. Through company performances, audiences can see the works of José Limón as well as new works choreographed by company members and guest artists. Through the institute, professional and student dancers can learn the choreographic works by studying with a select group of Limón experts. Most of the experts are dancers who have worked with Limón in the past. Using resources such as videotapes, labanotation scores, audiotapes, and photographs, they bring José Limón's and Doris Humphrey's dances back to life.

In the foreword of *An Unfinished Memoir*, Carla Maxwell, current artistic director of the Limón Dance Company, states "José's work has always been life-giving because it's so full of hope and harmony, even in his most extreme tragedies. He was letting us know that we have a choice that we did not have to act out our darker sides. I believe that this power and life-giving force in his work is what has enabled his company to continue these many years."

Glossary

avant-garde A French word literally meaning "advance guard." It is often used to describe artistic movements concerned with new and often shocking ideas that are generally not popular with the majority of people at the time they are introduced.

choreographer Someone who creates and arranges ideas and movements for dance.

critic A professional writer who describes, analyzes, or evaluates works of art, such as ballets and ballet performances.

dance composition The study of the craft of choreography or dance making.

heritage Something acquired from a predecessor.

jarabe A folk dance for couples that is popular in central and southern Mexico.

labanotation score A record of dance movement, similar to a music score, that uses notation involving symbols to represent parts of the dancer's body, direction and tempo of the dancer's movement, and the relationship of one dancer to another.

pioneer A person or group that explores new areas of thought or activity.

pure dance Dance that explores fundamental aspects of body, dynamics, space, or shape, rather than trying to tell a story or express a particular theme.

repertory The dances that a company performs.

residency A period of time used for advanced training in a specific field or art.

theme and variations A form of composition in music or dance where an initial statement is made in the first section of the work, then presented in changed or altered versions in the following sections of the piece.

to set (a dance) on The act of creating a dance or staging a previously choreographed dance piece with a new group of dancers.

For More Information

The Limón Dance Foundation
307 W. 38th Street, Suite 1105
New York, NY 10018
(212) 777-3353
Web site: http://www.limon.org

Limón Dance San José
c/o SJSU
1 Washington Square
San José, CA 95192
(408) 924-5046

National Museum of Dance & Hall of Fame
99 South Broadway
Saratoga Springs, NY 12866-9809
(518) 584-2225
Web site: http://www.dancemuseum.org

Web Sites

Due to the changing nature of Internet links, the Rosen Publishing Group, Inc., has developed an online list of Web sites related to the subject of this book. This site is updated regularly. Please use this link to access the list:

http://www.rosenlinks.com/lac/joli

For Further Reading

Anderson, Jack. *Art Without Boundaries: The World of Modern Dance*. Iowa City, IA: University of Iowa Press, 1997.

Foulkes, Julia L. *Modern Bodies: Dance and American Modernism from Martha Graham to Alvin Ailey*. Chapel Hill, NC: University of North Carolina Press, 2002.

Lewis, Daniel. *The Illustrated Dance Technique of José Limón*. New York, NY: Harper & Row, 1984.

Limón, José. *José Limón: An Unfinished Memoir*. Hanover, NH: University Press of New England, 1999.

Bibliography

Brown, Jean Morrison, Naomi Mindlin, and Charles H. Woodford. *The Vision of Modern Dance*. 2nd ed. Hightown, NJ: Princeton Book Company Publishers, 1998.

Cohen, Selma Jeanne. *Doris Humphrey: An Artist First*. Princeton, NJ: Princeton Book Company, 1972.

Dunbar, June. *José Limón: The Artist Re-viewed*. New York, NY: Harwood Academic Publishers, 2000.

Limón, José. *José Limón: An Unfinished Memoir*. Hanover, NH: University Press of New England, 1999.

Index

About the Author

Jennifer Cady, MA, is an in-school and residency artistic director with the National Dance Institute in New York City. She holds an MA in dance education, teaching in higher education; and a BS in dance education, K–12, both from New York University.

Photo Credits

Cover (inset), p. 5 by Arnold Eagle; cover (background), p. 39 © Photo by Gjon Mili/Time Life Pictures/Getty Images; pp. 8, 25, 26, 32, 42 © Jerome Robbins Dance Division, the New York Public Library for the Performing Arts, Astor, Lenox, and Tilden Foundations; p. 10 © Hulton-Deutsch Collection/Corbis; p. 16 © Condé Nast Archive/Corbis; p. 19 Photograph by Bouchard, © Diane Bouchard; p. 29 © Jack Mitchell.

Designer: Tahara Anderson
Editor: Leigh Ann Cobb
Developmental Editor: Nancy Allison, CMA, RME